HUMAN ANIMAL

Also by Anne Becker

*The Transmutation Notebooks:
Poems in the Voices of Charles and Emma Darwin*

The Good Body

Human Animal

▶◀

Poems
Anne Becker

Pond Road Press
Washington, D.C.
North Truro, MA

Copyright © 2018 Anne Becker.
All rights reserved. Printed in the United States of America.

Book design and Layout: Patric Pepper

Cover art: Special thanks go to the Bill Viola Studio LLC in Long Beach, California, for use and copyright permission as a courtesy for the cover photograph taken of Bill Viola's video titled "Man Searching for Immortality/Woman Searching for Eternity," copyright Bill Viola. Still photograph by Anne Becker.

Author Photo: Barbara Tyroler

ISBN: 978-0-9719741-8-0
Library of Congress Control Number: 2017959120

Acknowledgments:
Some of the poems in this collection have appeared previously in the following magazines, journals and anthologies, and online:

"From a Print by Maillol" *The Poet Upstairs: A Washington Anthology*; "Forces of Nature" *The Cooke Book: A Seasoning of Poets*; "Forces of Nature II" and "The World Dreamer" *Milkweed Chronicle*; "Passover: Part for the Child" *Whose Woods These Are*; "The Crack in the Earth" *City Paper* (Baltimore ed.); "Abishag" *The Washington Jewish Week*; "Work Horse" *Embers*; "House Work" *The Washington Review*; "First Scroll: In the Textile Museum" *Beltway Poetry Quarterly*; "Second Scroll: Chicago" *Antioch Review*; ". . . and there was light . . ." *Southern Poetry Review*; "Lament for Bob Dylan" *The Burgeon Book*; "Common Ground," "Mosquito Pantoum," and "Homage to the Globular Body" *The Sligo Journal of Arts & Letters*; "Fall, 2001" *Innisfree Poetry Journal*; "Not a Ghazal: Snapshots from the Museum of Life" *Gargoyle*.

The following poems were published in the chapbook, *The Good Body*, Finishing Line Press, 2007: "Out of . . . ," "Fall, 2001," and "I Spend My Days Among the Short People."

I would like to thank the editors and publishers of the above magazines and presses for first seeing the value of these poems which were written over half of my lifetime. I would also like to thank the Washington, D.C. area poetry community in which my poems were nurtured. In these difficult times, beauty, compassion and tenderness are so necessary for all of us to remain human. And my deepest appreciation to Mary Ann Larkin and Patric Pepper of Pond Road Press for their understanding of how these poems work together to create a whole.

Pond Road Press
Mary Ann Larkin and Patric Pepper
221 Channing Street NE
Washington, DC 20002
pepperlarkin@juno.com

Available through Amazon.com and other online booksellers, and through Pond Road Press.

This book is dedicated to my siblings:
in memory, David Becker, 1947-2009
—my mentor, my charge—
and
Katherine Becker Freeman
—my charge, my mentor—

Contents

The Poem Is a Story

One: Forces of Nature
    Forces of Nature • 3
    Forces of Nature II • 4
    Berry Hollow • 5
    From a Print by Maillol • 7
    Abishag • 8
    The World Dreamer • 10
    Passover: Part for the Child • 12
    Heartwork • 16
    Work Horse • 17
    The Crack in the Earth • 18
    House Work • 19
    First Scroll: In the Textile Museum • 21
    Second Scroll: Chicago • 23
    Homework • 27

Two: Human Animal
    Talk Music • 31
    . . . and there was light . . . • 32
    Wordplay • 38
    Getting Wisdom • 39
    Getting Wisdom II • 41
    Getting Wisdom: The Denial • 43
    Passover II • 46
    Lament for Bob Dylan • 48
    Beast and Man • 52
    Wolf Woman • 54

Three: Still, the Good Body
    Common Ground • 59
    Out of . . . • 60

Fall, 2001 • 61
I Spend My Days Among the Short People • 62
Not a Ghazal: Snapshots from the Museum of Life • 63
out of the engine of darkness • 66
Mosquito Pantoum • 67
Awakening • 68
The Old Loving • 70
Homage to the Globular Body • 71
Heartwork II • 72

Human
Animal

> *Then came the cat and ate the goat . . .*
> from "Had Gadya" a song sung at
> the end of the Passover Seder

The Poem Is a Story

of transformation, how
one thing becomes another.
But we never get over
what we first know—
that is, all the wrong
answers, misapprehensions:
Swedish great-grandmother—
she's Jewish—the half-
seen things: Angel of
Death rides the train
to Omaha, Nebraska
as she does—*one little goat*—
a child herself then, she
knew him by the glow
of his black skin.
Leukemia instead of
tardive dyskinesia: always
on the phone substituting
one word for another.
Now the ones with the answers—
the ones who have always spoken—
are going away, leaving only
a note saying, *Good-bye, I'll never
leave you*—erasing their voices
from the machine as they go.

One

Forces of Nature

Forces of Nature

Questions like: do angels have wings, these are the kinds of things
we demand answers to—and do they really fly into our dreams
with their array of doors, towers, baskets, rivers, radiators
and snakes just to show how we've been bad again;
don't they have anything good to say;
why do they appear in pillars of smoke, pillars of light;
are they afraid to show their face, or is the task
merely to keep us guessing—do they bite?
and how many of these infernal creatures are dancing
to beat the band on the stainless steel dance floor,
manic as usual at God's bidding, and why doesn't he do his own
dirty work, anyway, why doesn't he fight his own battles
and not draft us and his poor angels to blow until we're blue,
why do we continue to hope we were made in his own image
when all we know for sure is
we can dance like angels and we don't stop
whispering, "fools, what fools," as we float away

Forces of Nature II

This is the way the world is: the earth is served
to us on plates that ride on a layer of partially
molten rock. The possibilities for change are numerous:
the plates collide and pile up into great mountains,
the Alps, Himalayas—the light rocks of the earth's crust
pressed high into the realm of cloud and blue air—
or, the plates collide and one plate edge dives
under the other, deep into the mantle, the layer of hot,
heavy, molten rock—a water body cedes to the moving
mass of land, sinks into its own trench, and flows away—
in great rift valleys of the ocean floor, the crust
separates, a long crack pushed open by new, hot earth
boiling up from the core. We, and the earth we walk on
are never at rest, creating and destroying,
heating and lifting ourselves up into the blue air.

Berry Hollow

*As a flame blown about by the wind goes out
and no one knows where, so the saint released
from body and name vanishes, no one knows where . . .*
                                        Buddhist scripture

in memory, Richard Spector, 1948-2007

There are ghosts.
The civil war goes on.
Here, in the mountains, south,
it is not warm.

These rocks are millions of years old—
as long as the rocks remain
we will be restless.

The mountains are phantoms hiding in
trees and air, they are soft animals
sleeping and their sleep is just.

What's to eat? The berries are gone.
In the musty cabin, who leans over us
while we sleep? The snakes are gone.
Time drones on, loading and unloading its charge,
the tongue picked clean: *not this, not this.*

Herbert Hoover's bathtub behind the house
is full of empty bottles. Where will Herbert Hoover
bathe—at his retreat
on Graves' Mountain?

The print of cloven hooves in the meadow—

they scratched the dirt, ripped up the grass,
gleaned rotten apples from off the ground, there
at Clark's where deer have been.

Apple trees collapse even as they live,
so old and brittle, branches snapped in the wind,
dead limbs weather on the tree like barn siding—
it is as if the whole earth is rusting here.

There will be ghosts as long as there is air.

From a Print by Maillol

Picture the energy of rest,
the solid fluidity of sleep.
The scythe has stopped swinging,
a small detail hints that work
has been done, that this is an earned
rest and, of course, peaceful.
Her knees are mountains, her head
on her shoulder, her back against
a tree, propped on her elbow—
she cannot quite lie down.
But her body is wide and open,
few lines mark it off.
She is a prisoner of the tall grass
waiting to be cut behind her.

She and her world of grass are
sinking and she
doesn't know it.

Abishag

My lord, you are a marvel, an old
mountain rising from the sea—

but don't speak to me, your shaky
breathless voice will spoil this

night, let me see you as I will,
the old mountain, hard rock.

Yes, I am a virgin in the Greek
sense. I've come to give you one

night ripe with the old sense
of conquest, the fertile land

taken into your dominion—it's
easy for me to give this way—the soft

moist earth breaks under the plow's
blade—and I'm beautiful that way.

To ride your horse into battle, in the midst
of your brave soldiers. Young like

you, they loved you, your hard thighs
pressed your horse among theirs, you all

cried, wild for the sea and sweat, the smell
of death as your enemies fell screaming.

In the night, by the fire, you sang them
songs, lullabies to your brave soldiers

and your God, the giant's death. You
feasted with your men, tore the goat's

flesh from its bones as if those who were once
your friends were now enemies.

You were wild and happy as you never have been
since the war ended and the kingdom united;

I know, my mother told me how it was then.
But I'm young now, very young and small

beside you. They think I've come to save
you—to sweeten your bitter old age. Yes,

I'm young but I've known many men—
never a king, of course, since you're

the only king we've had in my lifetime.
Your flesh is slack over the old hard muscles

but you're a man for all that,
your wiry hair like stiff meadow grass,

your forearms are strong still,
you grip my wrists, but David,

I'm not helpless; hush—your face
is still beautiful and I love you

this way. In the morning I'll have
nothing to say. This mountain has been

crumbling for years and all your tears
can't move me. It's not fair—

if you were young now you wouldn't
love me and old I only love you in the dark.

The World Dreamer

The world walks through me in a dream—
I'm dreaming. Life is lousy.
But in the dream I start you again,
working a small plot threadbare.
When you feel each thread
it is beautiful, not like my brother
who is blue, his many arms
steal breath from his blood
so he tries harder. I'm tired
of watching him dance, all his
neon blue arms. There's my mother
or is it my sister?—in the dream
you forget—she tires me too,
the devourer, crusted with blood.
But there's more to the dream
than family, I go on to the next
hill, the purple and green earth
spills from my nostrils, I've made
young mountains old, bruised smooth.
Sky pours out of my ears, I think,
or is it that my mind is blank? In the dream
anything can happen but you don't
believe. My other brother
the elephant man, he's ugly, wrinkled
and fat: women love him when
I'm sleeping, I dream their love.
And my wife, the destroyer, in the dream
watches me sleep, my brother's breath
go in and out of me, blue.
She's more to me than family—
she's my roundtrip ticket, limitless
travel, my horse, the horse's
steel shoes, the ground they come

down on, fine dust, water I rain
on the valley, trees that grow
in the rain. But there's more to the
dream than rain and the smell of wet horses,
a man's wet thigh, his wife's beautiful
breast, their child's cry when they're sleeping,
I dream their love, in my world their dreamless
sleep. At last I remember the food—
how have we gone so long with nothing
for nourishment but rain? So I
dream food: good bread, my mother
just made it, the crust crisp, the interior
warm. And some fruit, make it
red. Make it an apple this
time too—but trust me this time.
Green beans, cauliflower, clouds spilled
out of the sky, squash blossoms, butter.
It isn't enough—remembering my sister I
left out meat—but this is the dream:
a few gas stations, trailer park, one brick
house, this is shelter in the dream, most
of the earth is desert. It's the brick house
where my wife waits for me to come
home from the dream, wet thigh,
my wife's beautiful breast.

Note: The first two lines of the poem are from a poem by Thomas Lux, "Just a Poem," which is a version of a poem by Dino Campana, an Italian poet (1885-1932).

Passover: Part for the Child

*If I could I surely would,
stand on the rock where my
Moses stood—Pharaoh's army
got drowned; O Mary
don't you weep.*

Again—again—
I turn into the
child, the boy-
king.

My sister was my mother,
my mother was my mother
and a woman, a strange
woman, at last, was my mother.

My mother put me in the water,
in the rushes. Did she think
the bushes would hide me, a baby
glowing red like light behind fingers?

I know the laws of nature:
water always parts, stems
bend in the wind and reeds
whisper. There are no secrets
in nature.

My mother pulled me out
of the river; she took away
my first boat. She called me
her child—I named my son
Stranger.

*Moses stood on the Red Sea
shore, smotin' the water
with a two-by-four—Pharaoh's army
got drowned; O Mary
don't you weep.*

I killed a man and fled, I hoped
to return; even his family might
forget in time—stone and blood
are not equal.

I met women with flocks that could not
reach the well—shepherds teased them.
I waded through the men, a path
opened; the women passed through
with their goats.

My wife's father is a man
of God—I should have been
wiser. It's not right for a child
to get mixed up in man's business,
and I was too young to be married.

He said my brother and sister would
help me: my brother is tall,
his voice can be heard in a crowd.
My sister is tall, she dances
and can carry a tune.

Again he taught me the Law:
a way to speak and patience,
to ask for what I want,
to return again and again.

He gave me a way with frogs
and insects; He made my legs
hard and my throat soft.
He gave the knife
to my wife.

He wanted the very heart
of me, my son, but my wife
gives up nothing
for nothing.

She would not let my son
go—she struck a deal:
"The child is mine, the skin
is Yours. He may go with the men,
but he will return to me in the end."

You can reason with God although
He is stubborn and tends
not to listen; He has his own
ideas about things but is

swayed by subtle argument.
I had my way with the lambs—
blood welcomes blood—and why
should this night be different

from any other night?
We went through the red
door and were gone,
when we arrived at the shore
it was dawn.

*One of these nights about twelve
o'clock, this whole world's
going to reel and rock—Pharaoh's army
got drowned; O Mary
don't you weep.*

Heartwork

This is my work. This
I love. My mechanical brother is
partner to this work: I couldn't
do it without him. But
my mechanical brother, his plastic
parts, electric parts, invisible parts,
switches, channels, condensers,

transformers let me down at each instant,
at every crossroad. He, who was turning
a moment ago, in a split second is still,
silent, withdrawn. Unlike me, he
can't stand up to the slightest stress.
Are we opposites? I am strong.
Steadfast. I labor, labor, labor

no matter how hard the earth presses back,
rejects the work of my hand, the changes I make.
But my brother, and I—see, I'm pushing, pushing;
he, a still point, stopped engine, mute—
we are both stubborn, we are joined by thin
wires, memories that diverge,
pictures that are the same but don't match.

Work Horse

for Ruth Rubin and Ruth Stone

This is my work. This I love. A willing partner,
I am tethered by an intricate system of
gears, levers, heavy wooden rods, to the millstone
that great blind surface that crushes all
that fall beneath it. That's my job. Look at this
solid body: taut muscles, gleaming curried skin,
massive feet, the horny surface of my hooves oiled,
shiny. This is beauty. This round and round,
daily grind, is itself a thing of beauty.
I am well cared for and I care for

my work. I pick up and put down my feet with slow,
thoughtless deliberation. Each nerve—each muscle
performs its appointed task as effortlessly as any machine,
contracts, relaxes, levers the joints and my foot
bends and rises, bends and rises, doing its work.
As I put one foot in front of the other I wonder,
is it me or the work that is the greater beauty?
You may ask in turn how any animal with a name like
Clydesdale, Percheron, Belgian Draft can make such
fine distinctions. But it is precisely this kind of

work, this wearing away, this refining
that leads me to wonder as each day turns into another,
as sweat foams like soap between my legs, a hot summer wind
lifts the coarse hairs of my mane, as little puffs of dust
rise behind me. Foolish people to believe
that hard, physical labor dulls the mind, crushes
desire, erases the idea of beauty. That's
just not true. I know. I speak from personal
experience: I was born a horse, a work horse,
and without me how can the earth turn?

The Crack in the Earth

It is better to grow fat on food.
The other hunger keep silent. So many
rocks cover over a crack in the earth.
The stomach alone cries loud, *Feed me!
Feed me! Cream! Butter!* Better not gorge

on lips and hair although we have both
in abundance, every day a new set.
How to ration love—we're not that rich—
so only a little for now, the rest
for the days to come when the supplies

don't get through. We've each
served our God well, holding back the
end of the world by sheer will,
so when do we get our medal?

Ah, fellow-soldier—or enemy—
remember the night we excited the water?
Invisible animals blinked on and off
when we broke the surface and the water
was warm.

And that night we climbed the rocks
at the place where our two worlds
were sliding by each other, and we climbed
down into the fault-line—now was that love?
Or were we just crazed?

House Work

How can we think to think this?
　　　　　Charles Wright, "March Journal"

I'm tired of making dinner, thinking of food,
the never-ending story of the dishes, covered,
uncovered, bacon, sweet potatoes, soup.
Ironing, flattening the fabric, making it perfect—
impossible task (I iron in wrinkles, iron them out),
thinking about the brain, that useful organ, better
than toes or breast. Tired of getting my son
to brush his teeth, to take a pee before bed,
asking my husband to fix the shelf in the closet,
the one that held my shoes off the floor, the one
that fell in the middle of the night two years ago,
woke us up but I was too tired to wonder what caused the crash.
I'm not yet forty years old and I'm that tired of my house,
tired of pretending no one lives inside here, tired of
picking things up, vacuuming crumbs, the mud we drag in
from outside. I want everything pure and simple—the way
it never was—when I was a kid and my mother didn't care
about dirt, spills, was ignorant of the cost of cleaning.
I have a picture of my sister still, fourteen, dusting shelves
while reading a book, the one time I feel anyone dusted
the house of my childhood—my mother's house—
we never cleaned the toilet bowl, in memory,
and we never cut the grass. Looking back, I see
my mother standing at the kitchen counter, preparing a meal—
we children seated on tall metal stools,
listening to the music of her talk.
I remember the first time, at age nine, concocting
meatloaf (my mother never did), getting the recipe
from my first cookbook. Or coming back from a semester in France,
demonstrating for my mother the proper way to cut a tomato—
I was a teen-ager still, cooking dinner for friends:

poulet provençal (chicken with black olives, mushrooms and tomatoes),
raspberries in Beaujolais wine. The thrill of it,
dressed up, table set with cloth napkins, no one there
but my friends and I. Now I'm tired of being adult,
of dealing in losses that mount up, draw closer
so that in the end almost all is taken away from us,
the vessels we placed our faith in—clean sheets,
dessert, the tart smell of Joy. The way my brother, schizophrenic,
is taken away and half given back, his brain ruined, the connections
wired in hard patterns (one wrong word and a terrible order descends).
My mother cutting loose from my father, wrecking the family of childhood,
new life for her at sixty-six. My grandmother's death—
she was ninety-four—the good rabbi spoke the holy language Gobbledygook,
I stood at the edge of the earth I think I know
and threw dirt after her like a curse.
What I have left is her cookie jar (which briefly,
at her death, transformed itself into an aluminum ice bucket,
but has again changed itself back). And her icon—
golden curved plastic bottle of Joy that stands on the edge
of the kitchen sink and presides at the cleansing
I still have to do.

First Scroll: In the Textile Museum

for Bonnie Lee Holland

In the museum, in the galleries' dim
light, long fibers hang from
the walls, fibers too fragile
for the scant dirt and oil of clean
hands, too fragile for clear incandescent
light. Fibers spun out from the cotton
plant, the banana tree, the linden, wisteria,
grass, the sacred elm, that have crossed,
have wrapped themselves around each
other, darted in and out, taken on color
or resisted, have formed themselves
into garments, undergarments, into bed
covers, into banners that celebrate
the woven life of the child. These cloths
fabricated on small islands in the east,
old pieces fashioned with new threads
into newer and newer work coats, sled-haulers'
vests, socks with split toes, aprons, gaudy robes.
On the back of firefighters' jackets
moon's rabbits stand up like men
pounding rice for rice cakes, head bands
around their heads, smoke clouds billow
across the shoulder's sky, lightning bolts
flash on the sleeves. On the inside
a red peony blooms like a torch fastened
to the man's skin. Bed clothes too:
a comforter mimics a robe, split open
at the spine, an extra panel inserted,
the sleeper has slipped her arms into
the coverlet's wide sleeves, back of the robe's neck
tucked under her chin—what dreams sail under the blue
skin of the sea? Where rabbits leap from curling

wave crest to wave crest, pale grey pelts
curling like foam, fearless, fool-hardy rabbit
wits that crossed the ocean from island to island
jumping from slick shark's back to shark's back,
jeering the living bridge before they touched shore.
Or foretell a large family, so many children
each separate, each joined by discontinuous threads like
foam, like watery spray, like the sharp scent
of smoke carried on the air. Or that bridge of
stars that spans a whole ocean of night sky, divides
those who love each other, through all these piercings,
these bindings, deep indigo field pricked and pricked
with light until a wash of light weaves a
road, a track, needle's path in the mind's eye. So that one
day, the seventh day of the seventh month, any
miraculous day, each year, they fly, they cross on
sources of light, they reach, meet
warm fingertip to fingertip in the blue air. Doors open,
we walk out into motes of red-gold November light.
The museum bursts into flame.

Second Scroll: Chicago

. . . a reminder of how it was
when they were human and you their child,
as though death had changed nothing.
           from "Signs" by Lisel Mueller

in memory, Jean Becker, 1894–1988

City of Shriners, pig slaughterers, incendiary cows, science,
industry—all necessary business. Becker's Surgical Supply,
my great-uncle gave up the soda fountain when he found
he couldn't make hot fudge sundaes the way he wanted
and still make money. Huge stone blocks hurled by exuberant
giants into the water at lake's edge, anemic
yellow rectangular brick houses hugging flat lots,
foursquare to the street, streets all straight, all
flat, running from the airport to that great body
of water geysering up in rhythmic slaps
at the end of my grandmother's street.
Sidewalks and alleys. The dry snore of skates
as we sped by mothers and children, shipping clerks,
insurance salesmen, custom inspectors, jewelers,
short order cooks. Hot dogs saturated with red dye
like red glowing inside silk, slashed with bright yellow
mustard, smooth and slick like crayon-color.
Grey wooden back steps that clung to each brick
apartment building (yellow, brown, pink);
dingy, angular, fossilized waterfalls, scaffolding
the sides of small sooty cathedrals, each
a house of prayer. Mornings passed sprawled
on my grandmother's golden carpet, a lamb sock
talking baby talk to a pretty ventriloquist, snaggle-
toothed dragon, little round-headed king. Endless afternoons
when my grandmother and great-aunt, seated at the
bright screen, invited unfortunate outsiders

who revealed deception, weakness, and muted
lust behind every bland face, into their immaculate
apartment smelling of sharp soap, pine oil, roast
meat, jello, garlic and toast. Unending jingles,
unending commercials, the bear water-skiing
through endless chains of lakes, touting
pig beer, a stomach admonishes a man,
his advice: moderation but failing that
a chalky liquid lurking in the murky
recesses of the top shelf of the medicine
cabinet of my grandmother's otherwise perfect
apartment. My grandmother, the one odd
Chicagoan out of ten, clicks on her up-to-the-minute
electric stove, matching pots electric blue. Freedom
of the city where we wander everywhere, on sidewalks,
through alleys, beyond the Roumanian meat market
Log Cabin, Walgreen's, the Jewel, the Gold Coin, Treasure
Island, Juvenile Sales, the old cemetery
held back from the water by two twisting
bands of concrete and a flimsy metal rail.
The same streets we walk in our styleless
bathing suits, to swim away from the city
as if out to sea and then back to the beach,
to shift pebbles from here to there—this is
exacting work—to capture only the finest
in shape and color as we were taught
by our mother, native of the city.
Buzzers upstairs release front doors, speakers
to speak up the stairs, courtyards, trains
gushing through tunnels, suddenly
in the air, stopping and beyond the window
nothing but air. Descending the electric
spine of the city, through the turnstile, ribs that
pass through ribs into the station, white tile
smeared like an ill-kept bathroom, broken

pavement, crushed curb. Then the giddy ceremony
of nails: my grandmother and her sister, their
chairs pulled up to the Chinese card table, with
grave concentration they paint cool flames
on their fingers, we half-swoon in the fumes.
And the solemn sacrament of cards. Again
the Chinese table, the slippery deck
rattling in our hands like bones. The dividing
into piles: hearts, club, diamond, spades; old
women and children alike dealt in. The deliberate
rhythm of canasta, quicker pulse of gin, slow
rites of war. And the ritual braiding of the fringe,
my sister and I hunched on the carpet beside my
grandmother's long celadon couch, our expert fingers
bend strand over silky strand down the entire length.
And the secret, fabulous mystery of perfume, my
grandmother's room, its residue, amber oil in
crystal jars, dresser drawers full of fake jewels;
mink coats and sealskin in cars crowded with human
bodies, soft pelt against cheek and back of the hand—
the skin drawn thinner and thinner, puffy blue worms
grow fatter. And the incongruous icon: my grandmother, young,
in a Gypsy's fancy dress, her black hair down her back
like a shield, satin ribbons cascading like rain,
mandolin cradled in her arms, an awkward weapon, one eye
scraped out of the picture, all held in the
heavy, ornate, gilt frame I gave her.
Now the last—the public—ceremony. The container
they closed her up in, high polish like a walnut
dinner table, rust flowers flare on the top.
And now the disturbed lawn, the cranking down,
the filling with dirt, labyrinth of stone.
At home—my grandmother's apartment—I wake
as always in the dark. Trace a slow pilgrimage
to the kitchen to check time without light.

Bare feet planted on her linoleum I listen to the sound
the apartment makes, her things, their
particulate hush. The peach bloom chair,
padded footstool on its little wooden legs
breathe easily in the warm dark.
In a milky glass jar her flame
burns all night in her double stainless steel
sink. It will burn until it burns
itself out. Perhaps it's a good thing
my grandmother is gone—she loves me but
she would not approve the way my hair
spouts from my head in flames.

Homework

When the doors close all words are prayer for the dead.
But the dead don't go willingly to heaven,
There being thick books they still haven't read.

So there in the dark, with one weak light overhead,
They strain their eyes to catch the last black letters:
When the doors close all words are prayer for the dead.

They take up no apparent space in our beds,
Bodies of smoke—no spine—they settle in our couches,
There being thick books they still haven't read.

Loathe to reach story's chill end,
Transparent fingers turn transparent pages with regret:
When the doors close all words are prayer for the dead.

But they hunger for words as we crave bread;
Devouring all: sound, meaning, shape, rhythm;
There being thick books they still haven't read.

I sense their hollow breathing all around my head,
Sentences and phrases, the praise they might have given;
When the doors close all words are prayer for the dead—
Their being—thick books I still haven't read.

Two

Human Animal

Talk Music

Two people who had been buried in the rubble
of a collapsed hotel for eleven days said they survived
by drinking their own urine and talking.
                from a radio broadcast after an earthquake
                in the Philippines, July, 1990

First time over the phone
        (we had not met),
in my concrete office-bunker,
        your voice in hand—
Don't know how but quickly
        we got to *death;*
told me when you were
        young you entered
a neighbor's narrow house, door
        open wide,
Nobody knows you—
dead child laid out in bed.
First time you saw
        anyone dead—
Where did our conversation begin?
(So many songs I know—so many
        I don't know yet.)
when you're down and out—
I, who was always shy, was
        shy,
You were not. I thought
I knew you then. What I knew
        instead
(brain so apt, fills the gaps of
        silence)
was your voice traveling the
        singing wires,
falling, rising
        in my head.

. . . and there was light . . .

still billions of years later
we try to find our way in the dark.

Today, a mile, two miles underground.
the men mad for discovery watch for the proton

to decay. They scan iron boxes, tanks of water,
that are invisible to them. Their eyes

bore through them, ignore iron, water, are
tuned to the billion trillion trillion

protons—the positive heart of the atoms—
so many the count means nothing to us

out here in the world of air, of
touch, of one thing after another,

the world that really matters.
Once we believed what mattered

was immortal. In church we chanted:
dust to dust, in school:

is neither created nor destroyed. But
there was always room for change:

loaves and fish, bread and wine, flesh and
blood, or burning—heat, light, gas and ashes.

But here, locked in the ghost world of wild ideas,
the men mad for discovery will do any crazy thing.

Gathered at sunrise before the shaft of the mine,
they wait for small elevators, miner and scientist alike.

The entrance to the shaft is a large hangar,
monkeys call from the rafters, mocking the men, warning,

"You fools, don't do it!" At the bottom of the shaft,
Hindu gods with their extra arms, their passions,

their soft rounded bodies, welcome the fools
who so blithely descend to the underworld.

In the Kolar goldmine, before a shrine of iron,
a cube of pipes, wired, charged with argon gas,

the scientist poses in red light. He is
demon-in-charge of the longest running

proton decay experiment in the world.
He is an expert in cosmic rays, he knows

their path, can disregard their trajectory
through his contraption. Like the others he has

embraced a grand unified theory; like the others
he is waiting for the proton to decay.

He thinks himself patient. Out of the morass of data
he has named six candidates for the honor.

He says, "Four are solid. We will stick
our necks out—no one else has done that."

Elsewhere under the earth, god's assistants
are working. In a salt mine near Cleveland, Ohio,

floating in a pontoon boat, watching
a pool of water, a man waits

for a wake of blue light to register
in his phototubes, solid evidence

that the proton has decayed. But the man says,
"No," as much as he wants it to the proton

does not decay. As much as he needs it to
the proton does not decay. "How can we exist,"

he cries, "if the proton does not die?"
In Japan, heaven on earth—where every stone

is placed just so, each grain of dirt—
in an ancient zinc mine, under those old volcanoes

we all know, in another pontoon boat,
in another pool of pure water, sits another man.

Let's say for the sheer beauty of the thought
that he is a Buddhist letting go, unthinking

his way to oblivion. For the job he has chosen
the largest phototubes in the world. The technicians

declare they are too fragile, not able to withstand
the weight of the water. He says, no matter,

fill the pool slowly. "Our data must be clean,
we need high resolution. We must be

better than our rivals." The air in his mountain chamber
is stale, hot and gritty. When a whistle blows

he begins his devotions. A true Buddhist,
he distrusts software. Seated

before a computer terminal, bathed
in blue light of the screen's unearthly glow,

his face empties of feeling as he traces
path after path the particles take

through his tank. He says it is all junk.
"This is a muon. This is a muon.

This is a muon." And every three days
a neutrino makes a change. When the proton breaks,

so in tune has he become to the angles of spray,
he can differentiate between the neutrino's devastation

and the natural death of the proton.
This is what he looks for, this is

what he wants. A true Buddhist,
he will settle for nothing less than non-being.

When asked directly he gives a non-answer:
"We will neither confirm nor deny but—

these events are not inconsistent with
a belief in the proton's decay." A true Buddhist,

he smiles when he says this. And, of course,
there must be an Italian in this search

for the true death of matter. An Italian,
in love with the physical, suave, supple,

elegant enough to journey underground and return,
gleeful, pleased with what he sees.

These days, of course, the dog is gone
but it is not as simple as crossing a river,

nor can we play our way back with a sublime tune.
In these heady days of superhighways,

of accurate maps, we drive ourselves there
in a car. The underworld is paved, concrete.

We are met at the entrance by the Italian,
our guide to Garage 17, our designated circle.

Chains clank and rattle; we are propelled
through a tunnel of yellowish grey fumes;

harsh lights light the way. At the heart
of the high mountain—result of the collision

of entire continents—the infernal machine
does nothing but wait, like us,

for the proton to decay. We are not
patient enough. We resurface empty-handed,

blinded by snow. Because we are physical
we have piled theory upon theory.

Matter, anti-matter, we imagine,
depend on each other, destroy each other,

with real protons, real neutrons, the winner.
Because we are physical we are bound

by what we know. Because what we have imagined
has already decayed (because we can't see it,

touch it with our hands, taste, smell it;
because we can't trap it, can't measure it)

the real too must decay, tiny particles smaller than dust
too must vanish, become nothing. Because we are crazed

by the thought of our own death, because
it pleases us, we pray the whole universe will crack,

fall apart, rot, vanish. That our own death
may be a small measure of the death of stars,

of planets, of the long-lived proton,
our seed, our mother, our god.

Wordplay

Your clothes are your toys,
my son says, as I don a striped
vest, pull on polka dot pants,
suspend half-moons—half black
half white—from my ears
so that we may rise through
night's blue spine. *Play*
is my work, my son
says, lays sacred word upon
word—I forgot to indicate
that we are free—burst
seed pod, small pebble, grass root.

Getting Wisdom

Although he is not yet three
my son waits for a delivery.
Although he has not ordered it
he believes that the UPS man,
that Childcraft knows he wants
a blue pencil box, his name,
Matthew (the wise one) engraved on top.

Our dog, the light dim in her mind,
bright in her ear, knows the whine
of the UPS truck starting up.
She alerts my son that again
today his delivery did not come.

Matthew does not worry for just such a pencil box
was delivered here once in his already
lengthening life. It had the wrong name,
Daniel (our judge), marked on it;
a present to be sent on to his cousin.
Matthew is forgiving. Parents easily
make mistakes. After all how else
will we learn? Matthew is certain.
His pencil box will come.

Everything is possible.
Once I bought him a plastic trumpet
he didn't even know he wanted.
Now he toots madly, Gabriel truly.
The dog dreads it like thunder, like doom.
Matthew laughs at the dog's fear. He holds
his trumpet upside down. He knows
what he announces will happen; no miracle
impossible; life one long virgin birth,

like a trumpet blast, whatever he wants
arrives out of the air.

Now he speaks to me of the dead.
The ambulance carries dead people.
The fire trucks, tow trucks, police car
pull up to the burning bookshelf.
I, who have so little faith, feel compelled
to explain that these vehicles offer help.
But he sees the news, he doesn't bother
with false hope for the accident victim,
the careless, the unwary.

Matthew sings, *Danger, danger.*
What is danger? he asks later.
So we discuss danger: something that hurts.
Sharp teeth, guns. He knows
blood hurts. Crocodiles are bad animals,
they eat their prey. We examine
dead squirrels in the road. Their death
is not his death.

In the meantime he says he will go out
and play with the dark—he is not waiting.
Matthew is right. We are all waiting
for delivery—from want, uncertainty,
from grief. A large red balloon
slowly rising out of sight.
Matthew is right. We wait.
We don't wait.
Something new each day.

Getting Wisdom II

> *. . . I recall what people meant by words*
> *like earth, sun, moon, stars and universe . . .*
>   Lyova Zasetsky, quoted in
>   *The Man with a Shattered World:*
>   *The History of a Brain Wound,* by A.R. Luria

Late spring. Late morning. Year One.
In perfect, balanced light, things are easy
between me and my son. It is before the flood:
he is dressed in the blue I love and what we want
is equal. (Oh—I am a good mother.) His padded car seat
protects him from harm. My son points, asks, "Wazdat?"
Points, asks; points, asks; begins to store words
inside himself. I see my son (transforming himself),
his miniature finger (vague replica of mine or yours).
I see the car door, would answer my son's command.
The thing itself is here—blue metal, white perforated
plastic, glass—I know what it is, what it does—
the light sharpens—I have no word to give to my son.
We all wait: Matthew, me, the finger, brain

I recall what people meant by words like—

door   door   car door

words join lips, palate, teeth, tongue and
pass over to my son

cat   juice   barrier   locust   mud

I eke out words one by one

stone   refrigerator   airplane   blood

axe   shadow water   bird

We are joined in combat.
We travel long distances at high speed
in a cheap blue metal box. Locked in.
We talk. Visit friends, dogs,
the house of death. But we are innocent.

forehead   map   thunder song

At times I am happy. We are joined by words.

spoon   rock   crocus   star

Late afternoon. Late fall. Seated in a shaft of light
my son traps dust motes in a glass jar.

Getting Wisdom: The Denial

> *... I hear my voice*
> *say, "No!"—the first truth ...*
>   Allen Grossman

1.
In the beginning was the basket,
hexagonal, of Chinese reeds and grasses.
My thought: Let's put trash in it,
bits of paper, a broken sword, string.
Mother-instinct to tidy the nest
so my four-year-old son could find his way
in the universe, among the constellations of
his things, Japanese dolls, imaginary engines
of war and high speed travel, blocks, plastic
men, car dealership in pieces.
My son saw the Chinese basket—lo,
it was good, *Put up a sign,* he said.
Dutifully I obeyed my son, for who
can resist the power of man naming,
even a small one in his own room,
without the skill in his hands?
This is a saving basket, the sign read.
And so, there are bits of paper in it,
scribbled notes, pretend money, twigs,
broken feathers, single beads.

2.
In the beginning there was nothing—
no—not nothing—never was there
nothing. In the beginning then there was
something and the something was without
form—no, it had no name. For a long time then
there were things without names.
Longer than you or I could tell

for there was no time then
there being no people to think
of it; to see our old deeds reeling
back away from us, in time, disappearing
over time's lip, memory's edge,
leaving us forever on the brink of
what's to come next, and nothing,
but then, there we were, we people,
and what came before without name
had vanished so that if there ever was
a time and nothing in it or
something without name, we didn't know it, but
before we could say I am we must
say: *not a tree, not a rock, not a bird,*
not a star, not dog, not light, not seed, not moth,
not air, not horse, not pain, not flea, not rose,
not blue, not lamb, not sound, not square, not death, not
fingernail, wall, box, hand, breath, bowl, hunger,
hair, claw, iris, blade, ape, grief, weed,
table, game, elbow, tongue, water, leaf,
leopard, branch, joy, fruit, pocket, ant,
lung, worm, root, mouth sun child man.

3.
Davy Crockett, gadabout and liar,
born in a bare cabin, close under the sky,
far from an ocean or lake, on the banks of
a sluggish brown stream—called in East Tennessee
a river—born like Athena, so he said,
already in command of the power of speech,
in a place of rocky red ground and rich
vegetation, mountains pushed up and worn
down, pushed up, worn down millions of years,
the smart talker, the one to make us laugh,
three-year-old bear slayer, mammoth tree-
child: my son's hero in his fourth year.

My son the smart talker, the one to make us
laugh, businesses are extinct, his wealth in bulbs,
teller of tall tales, angry when he's not believed;
and even before he could talk—raw pink amaryllis
bloom like a mouth. We read
Davy's own stories, religiously repeated by
labor poet and suave New Yorker alike,
in his reckless, bold language and we
read Davy's possibly true life in bald,
bland phrasing: runaway, illiterate, scrapper
who fought injustice, self-taught man.
In that book the end comes swiftly
in Texas without detail.
All the brave Americans died. Nothing extravagant—
nothing about Santa Ana, the funeral for his severed leg.
No, says Matthew, patient and wise,
all the brave Mexicans died.

Passover II

*And the woman conceived, and bore a son;
and when she saw him that he was a goodly child,
she hid him three months. And when she could
no longer hide him, she took him for an ark of
bulrushes, and daubed it with slime and with pitch;
and she put the child therein, and laid it in the flags
by the river's brink.*
Exodus 2:2–3

It was a strange day
    going and being sent
    away again—
All that time my body
    doing its job, the strong
    pain at my back, a
    river of nails—
Breathing, counting
    leaving the bed, water
    pouring down my spine
    lying back down, tiring
    there being no appointed end—
All those people I couldn't
    talk to, and the one
    I could, my mouth
    his ear—
And the very young man
    coming to me, anyway
    even though I couldn't
    hear, whispering
    inexplicably in my ear, saying
    his name—
Who took the baby
    from me, from the old
    doctor seated between

my feet, blessed him
with numbers.

If he cried then I don't
remember. Today, almost
a man—a man of
words—he says, "God
is a manifestation of
our fears." "Why did
God work in a roundabout
route: frogs, boils, the
river of blood?" His father explains
the importance of show. (Pillar of
light, pillar of smoke. Ocean
broken open.) "This goes against
my religion!" he cries. "Mother,
why did she say it's sad
I don't believe in God—that
insults me. *Smite*—
what a sweet word."

> *... as if he were holding the sea in*
> *his black hands,*
> *as if, after giving him all that power,*
> *she now could give him pity and consolation ...*
>
> from "The Same Moon Above Us"
> by Gerald Stern

Lament for Bob Dylan

Lament, lament for Hibbing, for Duluth,
      lament for Marquette, for Munising, for the Sault;
Let me lament the raw earth, its skin scraped off;
Lament for the grass pulled up by the roots;
Lament, lament for the pure child, the pure dirt;
Let me lament the sheer rain of words—each pure
      note harnessed to the right word;
Let me lament, let me lament, let me lament for the electrician's
      son with the sizzling hair, song searing the mouth, cracking
      the lips, lament caught in the throat;
Let me lament the swirl of ash on the tongue, the charred word;
Let me lament the eagle's beak rotted with poison, lament blowing
      through the nose, wind in a ruin;
Blistered tear, smooth cheek—let me lament the downy hair
      on the young neck, the suspicious eyes, the walking debt;
Let me lament the dumb repetition of hunger.
      faithful generations of want;
Lament, lament for the gate open and shut;
Lament, lament for the locked box of luck;
Lament for the rain both inside and out;
Lament for the money borrowed and stunned;
For the rank cruelty and unintended harm;
For the useless car and the wailing fire truck—
      for the *phony false alarm*—
Lament for the stiff mask strayed from the shelf;
      and for the electric son plugged in, playing himself;

For the risky kitchen where you freeze, where you bake—
    weep for real pain—the phantom ache—
Lament for the authorities, for the agents, for the brakeman,
    for the promoters, lament for the undertaker, the agitators,
    the commissioners, the free-loaders, lament for the sword
    swallower, the throat-borrower, for the war horse, the riot
    squad, lament for the scentless roses;
Lament for the pillar of salt corroding in the sun, he thought he had
    everything, he never looked back—he didn't know what he'd done;
And for wise incorruptible love—gone like ice—gone like air—
Lament for the quivering bridge;
Lament, lament for the angel visions of Johanna—were they hers?
    Were they his? Were they mine? Were they yours?
Lament for the harm done unto you, the harm you did;
Lament for the love done wrong, time mislaid, scratched
    face at the window, rain tracks on the pane;
Wolf moans at the blue door—jowl sagging, smoldering eye—his one
    song—his sole idea of order;
And woe sing the wholly free, released from the strings of the body;
Let me lament the busted windows of the sea;
And for the ship stalled at the shore, deranged harpoon,
    impostor cabin boy, manic crew;
Lament for the engine, lament for the sail, for the bowline,
    for the mast, lament for the whale;
And the delusional captain adrift in the dunes—
    his fevered pockets—his drunken shoe—
Fire thirsts, unquenchable, guzzling the parched air,
    tomorrow's long past, the hours rust—
And the little boy lost in the blinding snow, bitter cold, smoking eyelids,
    fire, the fire full of holes;
Lament for the north country, jumping off place, end of the
    world, mine's closed, the borderline's blurred;
For the bootless weatherman, the aimless wind—
    and for the *ghost of electricity* whistling its scorched hymn;
Lament, lament for the ground, insects that play there, delicate
    snake in the weeds, the purposeful ants, lizards,

turtles, everything that breathes;
Lament for the National Guard guarding the wrong door, for the bored slave,
  the *homesick sailors,* half-lit ladies, escape artist,
   crumbled fortress, cold Joker, traitor kiss;
Let me lament the strangled voice cut off of the vine,
  lament for the words that have shriveled and died;
Lament for the homeless, the ruthless, the witless, the clueless,
  the deathless, the reckless, the eyeless, the foolish;
Let me lament the pale night, the black daytime,
  lament for the feckless nickel, the friendless dime;
Let me note the little red hen's lament, and the evil step-sisters' lament, and
  the great ape and the little elves dancing their lament;
Lament, lament for this old man, his house full of knick-knacks, his single
  thumb, his dog Bingo, his nameless furious wife;
Lament, lament for the mutilated mice, the triumphant cheese, lone-
  some cornbread, juicy frog, the innocent knife;
Let me lament, let me lament, let me lament for the hoodlum persuaders
  of song—scattered dust—desolate carnival boys, their wild
  high-wire rhymes, their sisters' speechless science;
Lament, lament for the low ringing of the law;
Lament for the tambourine giant, the silver saxophones and the flutes;
Lament for Jack-a-Diamonds, for Gypsy Davy, for Mr. Jones "Don't-Know-
  What's-Happening-Do-You," for the cocky punks, the plucky
  scoundrels, the scorned lovers, the *jealous monk;*
Lament for the city of truth spoken in song;
Pity the shadow of the laughter of youth—burned—gone—
          their god knocked
  down—the ikon broken—rattle bag of bones and polka dot rag—
  already the prophets mourn—the robin falls mute—
  and the dove—and the raven—black fire flailing her unfeathered
  wings—their illegible scrawl—soft white underbelly of the brain—
  tick of the heart hung in its sac, roiling, swollen—
   golden drop of sweat;
And the windowsill and the tattered ceiling—
And the cowboy angel astride his cloud-horse, twirling his lariat candle;
And the renegade physicist fiddler, fiddling in anger;

Naked emperor at the edge, howling for his lost dominion,
His soldier-clowns stuck in their coffin phone booth;
And his junkyard bed, its skeleton mattress, his black tooth;
And *Maggie's farm,* what she grew there, her lunatic ma, her raging
        pa, her cerebral servant, her well-scrubbed floor;
And Rita and Annie, and Mona and Louise, all the saints in the penitentiary;
Let me lament for the 18, for the 30, the 50 years' wait;
Lament for the price you paid—what you had to say—what you were
        offered, what you didn't get straight;
Let me note every lament and lament each note:
                                    Let me lament
            the choked wind, the dry rain
            the shattered hand and the wall
            a shell, a shard,   salt   sand
            unmanned man   the endless highway's end
            lion's breath   footsteps silent   abandoned name ...

                    letmelament letmelament letmelament
                    letmelament letmelament letmelament
Ah mama, can this really ...
                        the golden bead of sweat

                        letmelament, letmelament letmelament

            letmelament, letmelament letmelament

Beast and Man

in memory, Zander Rubin, 1948-1985

We and our kind
are protected from so much:
in hunting season dogs wear red vests
to distinguish themselves from the wild
animals. So when violent death
breaks in on us through our thin tranquil
shell, we say, *killed—he killed
himself*—and understand little.

But we can't shut up, what we shunned
floods our lives like too strong light
or smoke, fear hums in our throat
a dread song. Squinting and gagging
we spit out *life* . . .
life, thinking to get it right,
stutter, *it wasn't my fault—*
what do we know?

We could have learned something
from that precocious toddler,
hundreds of miles away, years ago,
who points from her stroller
to the basset hound in the next line
seated patiently at the end of his leash.
Eager with knowledge she cries, "Look,
oh, Mommy, look, a beast of prey!"

Or from Simon, that great black dog with cancer,
whose death was predicted months ago, who lies
in an awful stupor of survival,
patient, content.

We could have looked at you then, patient,
at the end of your leash—but
what could we do? Hide
every object of danger: letter opener,

scissors, blades, all the household poison?
Early winter, your wife and I talked of hunters,
men with guns—they wear red to protect themselves from
each other. I was so sure then. "It's not right,"
I said, "They don't kill because they're hungry."
We who can feel sad or angry—the end of winter—
we still wonder (we know and we don't know)
what became of your

life, rich fabric, thin red
ribbon, small thread dangling, pull it
and the whole garment unravels. Your wife said,
"I won't let you hurt yourself," and took away
your medication. It was too late.
It was as if
you looked in the mirror and saw nothing
we recognize. The Beast of Prey

is prowling your cage with a mild, patient face.
I continue to think of that night—your mild
face—desperate courage—that
terrible last gesture of control.

Wolf Woman

If I don't wake up before she embraces me
I'll be the wolf she'll be me.
It's all my father's fault—he shut
the laundry door, locked the beast up with the wash
Fierce perhaps—but only a dog.
I fell asleep with the soft pad, pad,
pad of the wolf's feet inside me,
the staring head that weaves back and forth
in the dark—and now I feel
a woman's body next to mine,
smooth shoulder, warm thigh.
Cold gentle voice speaks in my ear:
I haven't slept in a bed in years—
nor has my tongue shaped human speech.
Gray-brown hair tickles my cheek,
ropy muscles twist over slender arm bones
that slide behind my back.
I left the ones I loved—my husband,
my young son—to run on all fours,
alive to what I could smell, ears cocked
to the smallest noise, mouse
nibbling grass seed, hare's breath,
soundless sounds. How human reasons
abandoned me I don't know, but like an unmoored
boat I have drifted far from that rocky shore
to follow compulsion's route—I go
round and round and can't stop—
even if I wanted to—and I don't.
Feel the scars, she said and guided my hand
along her back, over shiny ridges of skin where
she had been bitten by friends at play.
On and on she spoke, the silken growl
at my throat, delicate tang of rust

in my nose. Without sound
I circle the sheep round and round,
my neck stretched toward them,
my eyes bore through them, I am
need—pure—clean—I want to
eat—but it's not that simple—they want
to live, to eat the sweet grass. They bunch
together, a mass of wooly rumps, mass of
sharp feet. Are you surprised I
fear my prey? They move as I
move. I circle round and round, testing,
seeking the smallest, the weakest,
the one with the least
will to separate from the others,
its mates, its strength in numbers.
In the beginning this act brought
relief—but now I'm not certain—
now it's like work—like dirt—
blind white worm twists inside
me, it itches, the perfect
lie. Memory returns:
fresh pillow, easy meal.
Where did I leave the paths of
speech, the human fold,
to wander here alone? Can't
remember what I need: what is anger,
what's hunger, fear, greed. Now the sky turns
pale gray, the clover's black, wolf smiles
in her sleep. Now you must listen to me
wolfwoman, I'm caught
here, halfway between animal and human
animal, between go and stop,
between daylight and dreaming, between
predator and prey. My gray-brown hair stands
on end, I'm tired, I'm enraged
and I'm not sleeping.

Three

Still, the Good Body

Common Ground

What we love in common—the light: we'll say,
wasn't the light beautiful, the way it touched
the air, you gazing out your window,
me here, looking out through the leaves—
and dense bread, solid chocolate, although I
eat the bitter, you the sweet—and the clean
line of Japanese houses, their gardens of stone,
fountains of grass, raked gravel rivers—
and certain music, from the old mountains,
when strings vibrate like the wearing of stone.
And the son we made between us, tearing at
        the fault.
And all the words of the stories, crafted, laid
        down like a pathway.
Asleep in our bed, we both rage like stones—our two
skulls, side by side—rags of hair pillow our
        heads.

Out of . . .

> *Whoever has no house now will never build one.*
> from "Autumn Day" by Rainer Maria Rilke

The days cool to green and gold
all overlaid with sharp
blue, blue a satin cover
       of bright air.
Living pools in translucent cells,
the redbud fans its livid heart-shaped
hands, sun glints on the tops and under-
       sides of leaves,
like sun on the peaks, shadow in the
       troughs
of a vast green sea,
sky empty now of planes that stitched
       and cut the distance
in our roiling world.
Crows cry their harsh desires,
nuthatch mutter as they scour
       the lengths of trees.

And like cruel parents in stories,
we've abandoned our only son
hundreds of miles from home,
his bones pillowed in their bed
of flesh, crumbs in his pockets,
the only stuff to build
his own house out of . . .

       September 15, 2001

Fall, 2001

What we love in common—the autumn light.
Its particulate waves caught in the warp of air,
suspended in the hush between breath and breath,
a soft gauzy fabric to wrap our fears.
All around us the leaves die back, wither,
curl, set their blunt orange hooks in the clear blue
        air,
tapestry our eyes gulp in, life's wild thirst.
Plum dots of beauty-berry, cross stitched,
stipple a lime-green ground, dissolve in
        distance;
weave and flicker of wing and feather
nut-brown, cream, carmine, black, olive,
        heather.
In the shrill music of cicadas, of
the crickets, day ticks its final minutes,
dusk shrugs off its shawl of lavender light.

I Spend My Days Among the Short People

Pilot or poet?—to them it's
so obvious, so easy, *I'll try that,*
they say, *I'll just do this.* . . .
And I flit from miniature
desk to miniature desk,
pausing to look down
at the scrawled pages:
"Enraged," says one;
"Spiritual Storm," another proclaims;
"The Swirling Vortex."
Together we walk out into a silver-blue day,
watch snakes slip over powdery sand,
stroke the soft, iridescent scoop of shell,
recognize trash discarded by the sea,
debris, they name it confidently.
And one of the smallest of these short
people doesn't abandon me
when all the others dash off to the
next attraction, and we are alone.
"I'm afraid of death," she says, her voice
small in the big day. Short myself,
still, I am the taller person: so I feel
it's my job to push death away—
"But the tumors keep coming back,"
she says and shows me
fine lines of scars on her small
porcelain hand.

Not a Ghazal: Snapshots from the Museum of Life

Two women and a girl walk into the Sonoran Desert,
fish dangling from their hands—or are they umbrellas?

A flock of clouds sweeps by on out-stretched wings;
out of the cyclist's path a white butterfly bursts from the rent air.

A woman—her face heart-shaped—looks into her palm, an invisible
mirror held there, as she applies dark lines across her cheeks, her nose.

Fists of rain assault the dry ground,
send up small explosions of dust around droplet craters.

Framed at the window of a wattle-and-daub shack, a woman's face puckered
against the light—dark eyes, dark moons, under dark crescent brows.

Rivulets of juice run down fingerbone trails;
dogwood pleads after inchworm war, its naked arms upraised.

Dressed as if for marriage at sixteen, the girl is the negative of her grandmother,
dark dress, white hair, seated by the door, sunk into her chair.

In the museum I scan the glass cases, take away strings of words: "cloud scrolls,"
"Memory of Beautiful Women of the Green Houses," "tea dust" and
       "iron hare's fur" glazes.

Against an adobe wall, a man disguised as Death's Bride: white dress,
       ribbons in his hands
like a bouquet, human skull-faced mask, his veil held out like a gauze wing.

From pink blossom-wigs, mimosa wafts her powdered scent of woman;
the potato peels off her red tattered dress.

Beside a white painted egret, a boy poses, shark's jaw open like a halo
       around his head;
his arms crossed firmly on his chest, he knows he makes a strange apparition.

Ribbed clouds: sky's tongue strokes its upper palate;
grass' pale spider-fingers grip pink earth.

An old woman—a lifetime of hard work—stands before a scribbled wall,
one hand on her belly, one on her breast, she touches herself with tenderness.

Boxes within boxes, Joseph Cornell's windows on other worlds;
all exploration begun in the basement, Utopia Parkway.

A girl on exhibit, her bodice sequined, her skirt a satin fish-tail;
painted cardboard fishes swim in the air, suspended by string,
    around her.

Life's waste: lashes, stamen droppings, pollen nodules, tree's shriveled claw.
Dragon root, whorled solid river, golden furred flames, horned smoke,
    small green abortion.

A man in white, in a white cowboy hat, threads cautiously through
    a small graveyard;
the graves dusty mounds of dirt, wooden crosses with many arms,
    stones prop up the crosses, a pail overturned, and all across
    the photo's skin roll clouds.

Owls' mouths: the pod grins, laughs, scatters its life-jokes.
Bark blossom, bronze skull clangs with new idea.

A woman seated at a café table, cigarette held in her fingers,
her flesh barely disguises the bones of her skull.

Again and again he left them at Mermaid Avenue, went out for cigarettes,
returned months later. Now only his words are left.

A procession of women wearing women's masks, men wearing men's masks,
Death in his . . .

Chasing each other the birds fly in one of tree's doors and out another;
chicory catches handfuls of sunlight in her blue palms.

At a political rally, a woman strides through the street, her fringed shawl
    unfurled like crow's wings,
her black skirt billows like a sail, her white lace petticoat revealed beneath.

A lavender evening, early July, tops of trees turn
olive, then ochre in the animate light.

Two girls stand on the branch of a great tree—its bark the gnarled hide
        of a mammoth
creature—their skirts velvet, shining; their calves, feet and toes, gracile.

Night trees: a web of blood-red arms woven across the dark.
The cat, a white shadow against black grass.

Our Lady of the Iguanas, in her reptile crown, in her trillium-
printed dress; her face, her neck, her arms smooth flesh.

All day clouds pass holding hands—piled up, strung out, gauzy, billowed,
        cottony clouds—
and one small apricot cloud . . . trailing—an afterthought.

Two women, one with one leg, pace the dirt Pathway of the Dead to the old
pyramid of stones piled up in praise of the older mountain behind . . .

In the hush the worn wooden boxes make, we all unroll
from tattered silk casings our own repertoire of hope.

Now come all the blind portraits: Serafina, Doña Guadalupe, a gaucho—
their faces obliterated, obscured by smoke, dissolve into light.

If I could show you what *Anna* means, I'd bring you to the edge
of a perfect green rectangle, I would string words in the quiet air.

Note: Half of these couplets come from an exhibit of photographs entitled "Images of the Spirit" by the Mexican Graciela Iturbide. The other half come from daily observation, including a visit to the Art Institute of Chicago. Joseph Cornell, the American surrealist, did truly live on Utopia Parkway in Queens, as Woody Guthrie lived on Mermaid Avenue, Brooklyn.

out of the engine of darkness

shadow of foliage
the brown bear paw.
we have turned full face
to the moon, we reflect
its light. it tugs
at our bodies
our bellies bulge.
once more animals of the depths
silicon grains, we slip
through each other
dissolve
sodium—carbon—
the moose shambles
over the abandoned highway
crosses the solid yellow double line
dreams of flying
oxygen—helium—

Mosquito Pantoum

The insects and grasses await our demise:
a slowing crumbling of the concrete world.
Wild flowers hide beside the steps;
ducks watch from a tangle of bushes and vines.

The slow crumbling of the concrete world,
walls shed pebbles and sand.
Ducks peer from their blind of bushes;
we pore over our cryptic books, eyes fixed on
        the wild pictures.

Walls shed pebbles and sand;
a wild wind blows over empty sidewalks.
We pore over our books, eyes fixed on
        cryptic pictures;
ignoring our flittering, fluttering neighbors.

Wild wind blows over empty sidewalks,
sends glittery dust racing, tumbling—a cloud
        of earthy stars—glinting teeth—
ignoring their flittery, fluttering neighbors,
deaf and blind, crazed in this glaring space.

Glittery dust tumbling, racing—a cloud of
        earthy stars—
follows ancient man-made alleys,
blind and deaf, wild in this glaring space
where insects and grasses, beautiful weeds, rustle
and buzz as it passes.

Awakening

The body, awake in the quiet light of
early morning, watches—no, listens
with its eyes—as light touches
rice paper blinds, the scuffed wood
of the floor. The tender blotch of
shadow twitters like leaves.
Listens with its skin as the satin air
rolls in minute waves across the arches
of the cheek and stem of the nose,
riffles the hairlets of the upper lip,
swept over tiny bubbles of sweat.

Still, the good body, that woke and
slept, day after day, over half a century,
wants to crawl back to its bed.
To pull puffy covers up over itself.
Extinguish light. Foil gravity.
Nestle down into cotton, spun and
woven, fibers fine, white white like
cloud but flowing with weight like
water over itself, chilled by that
early air. To warm itself and rest—
still—to curl into its soft nest

so that its legs no longer need
to hold it up. Its arms refuse
doing, perform no gesture but twine
themselves around breast and shoulder,
the hands, barren, will burrow down
into the gorge of the chin, or tuck up
inside tufted armpits. It wants to have
to do nothing. Its feet lightly floating
one on the other, weightless like

chinchilla, or *kitten.* Bones held
together by hair. Each knob and

bulge finds a hollow to insert itself,
like a puzzle. Mound surrounded by
valley. Eyes blanketed by lids. Ribs
kneading the dough of the belly as
breath billows through lungs and slips
out of the shaft of the nose. At the core,
custardy brain, blue-gray, settling down
at the back of the eyeballs, over the dome
of the palate, behind the throat-cavern.
And the fibrous heart, muscular,
gargling, relaxes its fist.

The Old Loving

We come to it again, now old, loving.
Our bodies, cracked and repaired, ease
around still tender places. Fingers
creep over tiny pits and lumps that cobble
the back. Behind soft mouth, yellow
lion's-teeth. The penis, loyal beast,
resurrects its arrow of intention. Crumpled
tissue, splayed open, vagina pounces:
her desire—to devour it. Tough
spinal cord carries sense through
the *foramen magnum* to the brain.
Sucking and licking we nurse one another.
A great wind blows over the house.
The boulder of your head, my rock.

Homage to the Globular Body

from *"Femme se Coiffant,"* by Edgar Degas (c. 1881)

Three folds of flesh, belly pressed
between breast and thigh, float within the frame,
rich like those flowers of wood, leaves and scrolls,
gilt chains, golden fruit—could be pomegranates,
pears or apples—in each corner, that holds
a woman, her three folds of flesh, belly pressed
between thigh and breast, from tumbling backward
in slow motion, heels over head, off balance
as she is, into the curved arms of the viewer.
Captured by the artist's heightened eye—did he lurk
behind her on a ladder?—and sure hand and steady
wrist, pressed as the globular body has been
into the top left corner of the room, tethered
it rests, belly, thigh, breast, those delicious folds of
flesh, tucked into itself, soft rosy skin disguised in blue,
in green, in gray shadow, brush strokes feathered
on the underlying fabric, face hidden by
hair, arm folded into succulent wing,
hand holding a comb to the red, dark
strands that flow forward toward the
knees, nowhere to be seen, in shadow
stream of hair, even the shins rounded,
scoop of lower leg and foot, no blade of
bone to hinder the controlled flow of the
body into the air outside the canvas, oh,
if only the holding muscle at the core
where back and belly cleave, would let go,
we could take this body for our own.

Heartwork II

Think of somebody who loves you—
or loved you, but no longer here—
completely, generously, without stint:
the thought hovers around the heart
muscle, fibrous, tough, crucible
and chrysalis, live meat, fist
contracts, releases, squeezes blood
to the lungs, then sucks back its breath-
saturated blood, rams it out
to the hungering body which
loves generously, completely,
without stint, breath by breath by breath.

Enough effort—we can rest here.
Enough happiness for one day.

Colophon

The sans serif font used for both display as well as the text on the cover, is Myriad Pro, an Adobe Original font designed by Robert Slimbach and Carol Twombly, with Fred Brady and Christopher Slye. The warmth and readability of Myriad come from the designers' humanistic approach to proportion and detail. First released in 1992, Myriad is still a best seller and a designer favorite.

The body text is set in Minion Pro, also an Adobe Original font, designed by Robert Slimbach. Inspired by classical typefaces of the late Renaissance, Minion is a highly readable typeface, combining modern sensibilities with elegance, beauty with functionality, and versatility with old-style elements.

This book was printed by Lightning Source Incorporated in the United States of America.